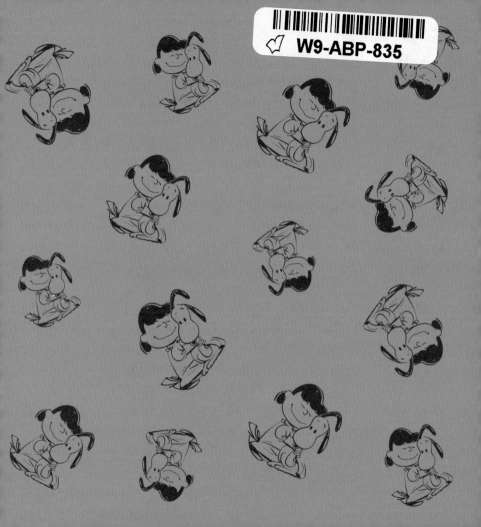

HAPPINESS

IS A

WARM PUPPY

BY
CHARLES M. SCHULZ

Happiness is a Warm Puppy

Peanuts © 2013 Peanuts Worldwide LLC

This is an officially licensed edition by Appleseed Press Book Publishers LLC

This special edition was printed for Kohl's Department Stores, Inc.
(for distribution on behalf of Kohl's Cares, LLC, its wholly owned subsidiary)
by Appleseed Press Book Publishers LLC

13-Digit ISBN: 978-1-60464-044-1
10-Digit ISBN: 1-60464-044-8

Appleseed Press Book Publishers LLC
68 North Street
Kennebunkport, Maine 04046

Design: Jason Zamajtuk
Typography: Clarendon and Arial

Printed in China
1 2 3 4 5 6 7 8 9 0
First Edition

Kohl's
Style # – 9781604640441
Factory # – 123386
Manufactured Date – 07/13

HAPPINESS

IS A

WARM PUPPY

Happiness

is

a

thumb and

a blanket.

Happiness is an umbrella and a new raincoat.

Happiness is a pile of leaves.

appiness

is

a

warm

puppy.

Happiness is an "A" on your spelling test.

Happiness is finding someone you like at the front door.

Happiness is three friends in a sandbox ...with no fighting.

Happiness is sleeping in your own bed.

Happiness is a chain of paper clips.

Happiness is getting together with your friends.

Happiness

is

a

smooth

sidewalk.

Happiness is finally getting the sliver out

Happiness

is

a

climbing

tree

Happiness

is

lots

of

candles

Happiness is being able to reach the doorknob

Happiness is knowing all the answers

appiness

is

a

night

light.

Happiness is some black, orange, yellow, white and pink jelly beans, but no green ones.

Happiness
is
the hiccups
...after
they've
gone away.

Happiness is a good old fashioned game of hide and seek.

Happiness

is

a

fuzzy

sweater.

Happiness is a bread and butter sandwich folded over

Happiness is knowing how to tie your own shoes

Happiness is walking in the grass in your bare feet.

appiness

is

eighteen

different

colors

Happiness is a piece of fudge caught on the first bounce.

Happiness is finding the little piece with the pink edge and part of the sky and the top of the sailboat.

Happiness is finding out you're not so dumb after all

Happiness is
thirty-five cents
for the movie,
fifteen cents
for popcorn
and a nickel
for a candy bar.

Happiness is one thing to one person and another thing to another person.

About Appleseed Press
Book Publishers

Great ideas grow over time. From seed to harvest, Appleseed Press brings fine reading and entertainment together between the covers of its creatively crafted books. Our grove bears fruit twice a year, publishing a new crop of titles each Spring and Fall.

Visit us on the web at
www.appleseedpressbooks.com
or write to us at
68 North Street
Kennebunkport, Maine 04046

APPLESEED
— PRESS —

— BOOK —
PUBLISHERS